Jesus
– THE WOUNDED HEALER

PERSONAL BOOKLET

DAILY READINGS: SELWYN HUGHES
GROUP DISCUSSION QUESTIONS: IAN SEWTER

CWR

CONTENTS

A WORD OF INTRODUCTION

IF YOU WERE given the opportunity to 'create' a new god, I wonder what kind of deity you might 'call forth'? Down the ages, mankind has continually been inventing and reinventing gods. Strong and powerful, mysterious, unpredictable, sometimes petulant, requiring punitive offerings, fearsome in appearance …

So, who is God and what is He really like? This is a question that many struggle with on a daily basis.

Some years ago now, a song reached the top of the UK charts with the lyrics 'God is watching us from a distance'. In this series, we discover that He isn't watching from a distance. God isn't just the God of heaven but of all His creation. We find Him, in Jesus, fully immersed in and engaged with our fallen world, experiencing what it is to be found in human form; suffering the same barrage of pain, prejudice and misunderstanding we can know. We explore together one of the unique aspects of the Christian faith, that its founder is One who not only sees our pain and suffering

but has also lived through the worst of it. We discover that the God of the Bible is so very different from the God of our best imaginations, and that He is found to be, as Selwyn Hughes has referred to Him, 'God the more'.

We may never fully grasp the mystery of suffering, but God does not leave us floundering. We can find that, though He may not take away our pain, He is with us in it. Jesus offers the example of how to meet suffering, and gives us strength and hope to face whatever comes our way.

Sincerely yours, in His name

Mick Brooks

FOR GROUP LEADERS ...

HOW TO USE

This resource is designed to include all you need for five small-group sessions. It comprises five DVD sessions, icebreakers, group discussion questions and prayers based on each DVD session and Bible readings to be used between each session.

PREPARATION

1. Watch the week's DVD session before the meeting.

2. Select the questions you think will be most useful for your group to look at. You may want to use them all, depending on the time you have available. We suggest you plan for 30–45 minutes.

THE SESSION

1. From Session 2 onwards you could start each session by reviewing how the group found the daily readings of the previous week. What did they learn? Do they have questions to raise? How did God speak?

2. Play the DVD and go straight into the icebreaker question, which is designed to get people chatting.

3. Use the questions you have selected.

4. Move from discussion into prayer. There is a prayer included in the material that you could use at the end.

5. Encourage the group to use the daily readings in the days between sessions. The readings expand and build on the topics covered in the DVD. If the group members are not used to daily Bible reading, encourage them to develop this habit. If the group members are already in a routine of Bible reading and prayer each day, you might want to discuss how best to work these new readings into their time.

6. On the last session – Session 5 – you might suggest meeting once more after the last week's readings to pray and consider the whole experience.

Jesus

HIS WOUN

ICEBREAKERS

• On an official visit, the Mayor of Leicester's trousers fell down in front of children from three different schools. Can you describe an embarrassing or humiliating incident that has happened to you?

• What are your favourite parts of the Lent and Easter season? (For example, pancakes, chocolate eggs, fasting, special hymns and services, Simnel cake, Lent studies(!), visiting relatives etc.)

FOR GROUP DISCUSSION

• Talk about the ways in which Christ humbled Himself.

...SWER OUR WOUNDS

- Why did Christ allow Himself to be humbled?

- What is the difference between real and false humility?
  (For example, consider Uriah Heap!)

- How can Christians demonstrate humility?

- What does Christ's humility reveal about the character
  of God?

• Why can Jesus deal with us so gently and effectively?
  (See Hebrews 2:9–18; 5:1–10.)

• Discuss the quote of Edward Shillito from 'Jesus of the Scars':

  The other gods were strong, but Thou becamest weak
  They rode, but Thou didst stagger to a throne
  But to our wounds only God's wounds can speak
  And not a god has wounds, but Thou alone.

PRAYER

Jesus, I thank You that You are not a God watching from a distance but that You humbled Yourself and by taking on human flesh experienced all our weaknesses and suffering. You are truly a wounded and wonderful Saviour. Amen.

*Edward Shillito, *Jesus of the Scars and Other Poems* (London: Hodder & Stoughton Ltd, 1919). Reproduced by permission.

PITY, SYMPATHY AND EMPATHY

FOR READING AND MEDITATION – LUKE 24:36–53

'It is I myself! Touch me and see; a ghost does not
have flesh and bones, as you see I have.' (v.39)

WE WILL BE meditating on the truth that Jesus is not just a healer, but a *wounded* healer. He is able to help us with our hurts because He has experienced our hurts and by reason of this, He is able, as the old hymn puts it, 'to soothe our sorrows and heal our wounds'. One of the definitions of Christianity I have come to appreciate is this: 'Christianity is that religion which puts a face and flesh on God.' Suppose there were no flesh in the Godhead, no face like our face – would the Godhead be attractive and approachable? Could we come to God in confidence, knowing that He truly understands? Hardly. He would certainly be able to understand our condition from an objective viewpoint, but He would not have been able to empathise with us, for empathy flows only from involvement.

There are three main words used to describe the action of feeling for someone who has been hurt or wounded – pity, sympathy and empathy. Pity is feeling *for* someone; sympathy is feeling *like* someone; empathy is feeling *with* someone. Pity says: 'There, there, don't cry.' Sympathy says: 'I will cry with you.' Empathy says: 'It really hurts. I have cried those same tears too, but let me be with you and together we can find hope and strength to deal with them.' There is a small degree of pity and sympathy to be found in all true empathy, but the thing that makes empathy so much more helpful is that while it feels so deeply, it is able to identify with the hurt and draw alongside without being overcome with the plight of the person. Our Father's heart is like this; His sojourn among us enables Him to feel, not only *for* us and *like* us, but *with* us.

Blessed Lord Jesus, I come to You with thanksgiving in my heart for the fact that You meet me in the midst of my need. You have lived amid my needs and thus You can feel for me in my needs. I am so deeply, deeply grateful. Amen.

'IT LAYS NO HOLD ON MY HEART'

FOR READING AND MEDITATION – JOHN 3:1-17

'For God so loved the world that he gave
his one and only Son …' (v.16)

WE CONTINUE WITH the thought we touched on yesterday: suppose there were no flesh in the Godhead, no face like our face – would the Godhead be attractive and approachable? If God had just given us the principles for living without having put Himself in our condition, those principles would have made little impact on our lives.

Take the statement: 'A new command I give you: Love one another. As I have loved you, so you must love one another' (John 13:34). The thing that gives this statement such power is the phrase *'As I have loved you'*. The principle of loving has been exemplified in a person – and a person who is not just like God, but is like us. Principles are powerful, but they become even more powerful when they are expressed through a person. Suppose a child is crying for its mother and you say, 'Don't cry, little child. Take comfort that there is a principle in this world called the principle of motherhood.' The child would continue to sob, 'But I want my mother.'

The great Indian poet Tulsidas, when contemplating the many gods of India and realising how unable they were to understand what went on in the inner depths of his being, said, 'The Impersonal lays no hold on my heart.' The Impersonal is too cold and unresponsive. The principles of living become power only as they are embodied in a person, and in a person who is not immune to the sufferings and woes that plague the human condition. Otherwise those principles fall faintly upon the human heart. God has given us more than principles; He has given us Himself. Now He knows us – from within.

Father, I am bowed in wonder as I contemplate the idea that You thought so much about my condition that You would not rest until You had tasted my condition. My person responds to Your Person. Blessed be Your name for ever. Amen.

GOD'S CREDIBILITY RATING

FOR READING AND MEDITATION – JOHN 1:1–18

'And the Word became flesh and dwelt among us, and we beheld his glory ... full of grace and truth.' (v.14, NKJV)

DR CYNDDYLAN JONES, one of Wales' greatest revival preachers and a famous theologian, once said, 'The only way for God to maintain His credibility in the midst of a human race that was ravaged by sin was to taste for Himself the conditions under which we live. This He did in the act of the Incarnation, and so before He gave Himself *for* us, He gave Himself *to* us.'

Powerful words, but the text before us today puts it even more powerfully: 'The Word became flesh and dwelt among us.' I love the phrase: *'and dwelt among us.'* The visit of God to our world was not a momentary rift in the clouds, giving us just a fleeting glance of the Deity. No, He *dwelt* among us, from the manger to the tomb; amid our poverty, amid our temptations, amid our problems and our choices, amid our oppositions and disappointments.

Thirty-three years on planet Earth was not long, but it was certainly long enough for Him to sweep aside all charges that might be levelled against Him by both unbelievers and sceptics that God was aloof and insensitive to the plight of His creation. He met life as you and I meet it. He called on no spiritual power not at our disposal for His own moral struggles. He performed no miracle to extricate Himself from any difficulty. He had power to restrain power, holding it only for the meeting of human need in others. He never performed a miracle just to show power or confound an enemy. And don't think (as many do) that because He was God in human form, His divine nature prevented Him from feeling just as keenly as we do the hurts and sorrows that from time to time are the experience of every single one of us. He feels for us because He has felt like us.

O Father, help me to snuggle up to Your heart today and contemplate the wonder of the fact that You are a God who knows exactly how I feel. Believing – I nestle. Amen.

COME BOLDLY ...

FOR READING AND MEDITATION – HEBREWS 5:1–14

'Although he was a son, he learned obedience
from what he suffered.' (v.8)

WE CONTINUE DISCUSSING the point that because Christ has worn our flesh and has experienced the conditions under which we live, He is able to enter into our sufferings and our sorrows in a real and personal way. It is because of this that the writer of the book of Hebrews bids us to 'come *boldly* to the throne of grace, that we may obtain mercy and find grace to help in time of need' (Heb. 4:16, NKJV, my emphasis).

Over the years I have been astonished at the way in which this text has been misused and misapplied. I have sat in many prayer meetings in my time and heard Christians pray something like this: 'Father, we are thankful that we don't have to tiptoe into Your presence, but as Your Word says, we can come *boldly*. And we come boldly because the veil has been torn away and there are no obstacles on our path to the eternal throne.'

Now I have no problem with these or similar expressions, and I'm sure God doesn't either, but when I hear them I wonder whether those who refer to this text really understand what it is saying. We are encouraged to come *boldly* to the throne of grace, not just because the way has been opened up for us, but because One sits on the throne who knows exactly how we feel. The thought in the text is this: Don't stand there timidly, hesitantly, fearfully – wondering whether God really understands what is going on inside you or not. He knows and feels and cares. He knows the whole gamut of your human emotions. He knows you better than you know yourself. And so come into His presence boldly; He really is a sympathetic and understanding God. Can anything be more wonderful on earth or in heaven?

O Father, the more I ponder the truth that You know everything I feel, the more my heart bows in awe before You. Your understanding helps me stand. I am so grateful. Amen.

'THE COMFORTING CHRIST'

FOR READING AND MEDITATION – ISAIAH 53:1–12

'A man of sorrows and acquainted with grief.' (v.3, NKJV)

TODAY WE EXAMINE a question which is often asked by those passing through deep emotional trauma: how can the Christ enter into my feelings when He did not experience the same kind of situation I am going through at present? A man once said to me when I tried to offer him support and comfort at the death of his three-month-old baby, 'Jesus didn't know what it was to lose a child, for He was never a father. How can He really understand what my wife and I are feeling at this moment?'

My response was this: although the problems we face in our world are varied and different, those problems produce a pain in our heart that is shared in the same way by everyone. I asked, 'How would you describe the pain you are feeling in your heart at this moment?' Without hesitation he replied, 'Desolating grief and sorrow.' I shared with him that although Christ had not passed through the identical circumstances through which he and his wife had just passed, He most certainly had felt, and felt equally keenly, the pain of 'desolating grief' which was going on in his heart. This truth appeared to comfort him as it has comforted many others with whom I have shared it. I hope it might comfort you today.

The problems on the surface of our lives may have different wrappings, but deep down in our hearts the pain we experience has the same labels – hurt, sadness, grief, emptiness, despair, disappointment. The problems in our world lead to pain in the heart and it is *that* pain, whatever its label, that Christ has touched somewhere on the journey between His birth and His death. No wonder our Lord is referred to by so many as 'the comforting Christ'.

Jesus, my blessed Redeemer, I thank You that You know and understand every pain I may feel. My pains are Your pains. This makes You more than just the 'Truth'; it makes You the warm, tender, compelling Truth. I am eternally grateful. Amen.

Jesus 'WHY HAV

ICEBREAKER

Describe, if possible, a time when you have felt lonely –
and try to identify your specific feelings.

FOR GROUP DISCUSSION

• Consider the suggestion that loneliness is a sin.

• What does the Trinity of Father, Son and Holy Spirit reveal?

• Why did God create Eve? (See Genesis 2:15–25.)

OU FORSAKEN ME?'

- What are the causes of loneliness and how may it be self-inflicted?

- Is it possible for a Christian never to feel lonely?

- What loneliness did Jesus experience?

- Consider Christ's 'cry of dereliction' from the cross,
  'My God, my God, why have you forsaken me' (Matt. 27:46).

PRAYER

Lord, I worship You because You do not just offer us heavenly wisdom but the sympathy and understanding that comes from earthly experience. I thank You, too, that You sent another companion for us – the Holy Spirit. Amen.

NEVER FORSAKEN

FOR READING AND MEDITATION – HEBREWS 13:1–15

'For he himself has said, "I will never leave
you nor forsake you."' (v.5, NKJV)

I WANT NOW to focus your attention on a feeling which Christ experienced that I hope you will never know, but which nevertheless you may encounter at some point in your life. I have in mind the experience of feeling abandoned and forsaken by God. Perhaps no feeling is as intolerable and disabling as that of feeling deserted by God. But even this darkest of dark hours our Lord knows. His piteous cry of dereliction on the cross makes Him kin to all those who feel themselves deserted by the Almighty, and of course His glorious resurrection (we must not forget that) proves beyond all cavil that

Behind the dim unknown
Standeth God within the shadow
Keeping watch above His own.

James Russell Lowell (1819–1891)

All men to whom is entrusted the care of souls are familiar with fine Christian people who, at times, feel their prayers go unheeded or who pray for something that seems of certainty to be within the will of God and yet find the 'heavens as brass', and thus are tempted to believe that God has forgotten or abandoned them. It must be made clear right at the outset, however, that although a Christian may feel abandoned by God, the feeling is the result of illusion, not reality. We are never really abandoned, even though we may feel abandoned. He could no more abandon one of His blood-washed children than He could tell a lie!

O Father, let the wonder of this fact sink deeply into my spirit – that no matter what my feelings tell me, the truth is that I am Yours for eternity. You forsook Your Son in order that You might not forsake me. Thank You, dear Father. Amen.

'THE DARK NIGHT OF THE SOUL'

FOR READING AND MEDITATION – MATTHEW 27:45–54

'My God, my God, why have you forsaken me?' (v.46)

ALL MEN TO whom is entrusted the care of souls are familiar with people who feel forsaken by the Lord. When I first entered the Christian ministry, I remember being deeply perplexed by the fact that, from time to time, I would meet good and sincere Christians who told me they felt deserted by God. I remember walking on the Welsh mountains one day in company with a well-known evangelist, a man greatly used of God, who confessed to me that he felt that God had abandoned him. His confession shook me to the depth of my spiritual foundations. I wondered how it could be that a man so close to God could feel forsaken by Him.

I have not gone through an experience like that myself, but I have known hundreds who have. J.B. Phillips, best known for his translation of the epistles into modern English, *Letters to Young Churches*, which he subsequently extended to a translation of the whole New Testament, went through such an experience. His wife Vera, and a close friend Edwin Robertson, compiled a selection of letters he wrote which reveal the pain he underwent as he passed through what theologians call 'the dark night of the soul'.

Dr Leslie Weatherhead, previously minister of the City Temple, London, tells of a similar experience also. In a letter to J.B. Phillips, he said, 'I felt concerned about what you describe ... because I went through the same hell thirty years ago.' Teresa of Avila knew the experience too. In fact, Christian history is filled with the record of men and women who went through 'the dark night of the soul'. It happens to the choicest saints – something you ought to struggle to remember should it ever happen to you.

O Father, I feel today as Your Son must have felt when He prayed, 'let this cup pass from me'. Help me to understand this strange phenomenon, so that either it will not overtake me or I shall be adequately prepared to meet it. In Jesus' name. Amen.

PHYSICAL AFFECTS SPIRITUAL

FOR READING AND MEDITATION – 1 THESSALONIANS 5:12–28

'May your whole spirit, soul and body be kept blameless
at the coming of our Lord Jesus Christ.' (v.23)

WE CONTINUE LOOKING at the issue of deeply committed Christian men and women experiencing times when they feel as if God has abandoned them. How can this be? If God is wanting to have fellowship with them and they are wanting to have fellowship with God – what hinders the meeting? Why is there no sense of 'getting together' – no close communion? From our understanding of Scripture the problem is not in God, therefore it must be something unsuspected in them. If they are not deliberately indulging in some known sin, or consciously resisting God at some point where He has a plain controversy with them, the barrier must be hidden.

Sometimes the barrier is a fault in the person's physiology. When something goes wrong with our physical functioning, it can soon affect our inner condition and make us feel spiritually bereft. Elijah is a case in point. This great man of faith came to a time when he wanted to die: 'I have had enough, Lord … Take my life …' (1 Kings 19:4), but part of his problem lay in the fact that he was overtired and overworked. He had been busier than he should have been, so God had to slow him down so that his body could catch up with his spirit.

In my time, I have dealt with literally hundreds of people whose low spiritual condition was influenced by a physical malfunction such as a glandular problem, a viral infection or some other type of chemical disturbance. In many of these cases, proper medication was all that was needed to restore the body to a position of balance, and thus take pressure off the soul. Never forget that the physical can deeply affect the spiritual.

Father, help me to see that You have made me in such a way that what affects me on the outside can affect me on the inside – and vice versa. Give me wisdom to take this into account when next I am feeling spiritually low. In Jesus' name. Amen.

TELLING YOURSELF THE TRUTH

FOR READING AND MEDITATION – ROMANS 12:1–13

'Do not conform any longer to the pattern of this world,
but be transformed by the renewing of your mind.' (v.2)

WE SAW YESTERDAY how faulty physical functioning can affect our spiritual condition and bring about the feeling that God is not interested in us or is far away. This feeling can also be brought about through psychological malfunctioning, such as having a faulty concept of God, unrealistic expectations, perfectionist standards, irrational fears and so on. In fact, J.B. Phillips (to whom we referred earlier on) kept a diary of the thoughts that went through his head day by day, and found on reflection that they were almost all filled with negativism and gloom.

Here is a list of some of those thoughts taken directly from his diary, which, as you see, come across as rambling and confused: 'Seems I cannot get rid of colossal fantastic demands'; 'Have discovered my own limitations but still feel the demand to give 130 per cent'; 'Rather die than be ordinary'; 'The centre of my worship and my energies is – I'll show them'; 'The God I have been looking for is not a grown-up God at all'; 'I want to be colossal or soon die'; 'If I left the world a great light would go out'; 'Nearly all that I call God is my father magnified'.

Is it any wonder then, with thoughts like those buzzing around in his head, that God seemed to be far away? When the feeling of being abandoned by God comes mainly from the thoughts in our heads, then good Christian counselling can show us how to deal with them. Take my advice, if you cannot solve this problem yourself, discuss the issue with a mature Christian friend.

Father, help me to understand how what I tell myself greatly influences and affects the way I will feel. Teach me how to stop believing lies and believe the truth. In Jesus' name. Amen.

For those who struggle with troublesome thoughts, CWR recommends Selwyn's book *Christ Empowered Living* and Clare Blake and Chris Ledger's *Insight into Anxiety*, both published by CWR.

THE CRY OF DERELICTION

FOR READING AND MEDITATION – PSALM 22:1–24

'My God, my God, why have you forsaken me?' (v.1)

TODAY WE LOOK in detail at an issue which I touched on a few days ago – 'the cry of dereliction'. The phrase is used by theologians to describe the feelings of abandonment which our Lord appeared to have had when He cried out from the cross: 'My God, my God, why have you forsaken me?'

Throughout the history of the Church, great debates have taken place on this matter of Jesus' cry of dereliction. Some believe He was not actually abandoned by God but felt abandoned, while others take the view that it was much more than a feeling and that on the cross He actually was forsaken by God. I find myself in agreement with the latter of these two beliefs. R.W. Dale, in his book *The Atonement*, convinced me of this when he wrote, 'I decline to accept any explanation of these words which implies that they do not represent the actual truth of our Lord's position. I cannot believe that Jesus was uttering a false cry.'

Just imagine it – our Lord, who had been forsaken by men, was now being forsaken by God. As He began to experience in His soul the suffering of sin (not His own sin, but ours) and proceeded through His sufferings to pay the terrifying debt that sin had built up in the universe, God, who could have nothing to do with sin, had to turn His back on Him. Jesus plunged into the darkness of sin and endured the awful suffering of the atonement entirely on His own. He experienced on the cross not just a felt, but a real abandonment – something those who are Christians will never experience. Let this solemn but glorious truth take hold of you today – because He was abandoned, you will never be abandoned.

O Jesus, my Lord and God, I bow my head and heart in deepest gratitude for the fact that You were willing to be forsaken by God so that I might be at one with Him for ever. May my life reflect this gratitude, not just today but every day. Amen.

Jesus MISUNDERS

ICEBREAKER

Do you agree with the saying, 'Sticks and stones may break my bones but words will never hurt me'? Can you give examples from your own life?

FOR GROUP DISCUSSION

• Consider how the ABC theory applies to a farmer in a drought and a bride on her wedding day when the weather forecast is for rain.

• Why do words alone carry such power over our lives?

) AND CRITICISED

- At what times did Jesus experience unjust criticism and misunderstanding (eg Matt. 13:54–57)?

- How did Jesus respond to criticism and misunderstanding?

- What is the difference between constructive and destructive criticism and how should we handle each type?

- Describe how we might harbour a hurt and what the effects would be.

- How have you been hurt by other people's words or even your own destructive self-criticism? What should you do to release the poison of bitterness or inferiority from your system?

PRAYER

Dear Jesus, how You must have been stung by misunderstanding and unjust criticism. Yet You responded with forgiveness, grace and revelation. May I respond in the same way. Amen.

'THE PARALYSING STING OF HUMANITY'

FOR READING AND MEDITATION – MATTHEW 8:18–27

'But Jesus told him, "Follow me, and let the
dead bury their own dead."' (v.22)

JESUS NOT ONLY knew what it was to be criticised, He also knew what it was to be misunderstood. Few things are more difficult to live with than being misunderstood. Sometimes it's downright unbearable. One author calls it 'the paralysing sting of humanity'. When I first read that description, I felt the writer was overstating the issue, but the more I have thought about it, the more I have come to agree. When you are misunderstood, you have no defence.

Perhaps you have been in such a situation recently – or you may be passing through such a phase at this very moment. Have you noticed how when you are misunderstood, no matter how hard you try to correct the misunderstanding, it doesn't seem to get you anywhere? Usually, it gets worse. You get all your facts lined up, ready to make things clear, and all you get are blank looks of incredulity and unbelief. The harder you work to make your motives clear, the worse it gets and the deeper it hurts. Yes, the sting of being misunderstood can be truly 'paralysing'. I don't think there is a person alive who has not at some time or another felt misunderstood.

When analysed, misunderstanding can be seen as having two elements: one, an innocent remark or statement that is misinterpreted, and two, the offence that arises in the heart of another due to the mistaken interpretation. Jesus was constantly being misunderstood. Every statement and utterance that fell from His lips came from a heart of love, but still He was misinterpreted and thus maligned. Believe me, no one knows better than Jesus what it means to be misunderstood.

Loving heavenly Father, once again I want to express my thanks for the fact that when I am misunderstood, You not only know how I feel but can help me keep my spirit intact. I am deeply, deeply grateful. Thank You, dear Father. Amen.

LEARNING HOW TO BE A KING

FOR READING AND MEDITATION – 1 SAMUEL 16:1–13

'So Samuel took the horn of oil and anointed him and
… the Spirit of the Lord came upon David …' (v.13)

YESTERDAY WE SAW that misunderstanding can arise from
an innocent word or implication. Nothing was meant by it, but it
was misread and an offence was created. Apart from Jesus, one of
the most misunderstood men in Scripture was King David, and
a brief examination of his life will illustrate for us the dynamics of
misunderstanding. After David had been anointed with oil by Samuel,
the statement was made to Jesse's family: 'Your youngest is going to be
king.' But learning how to be king included learning how to endure
being misunderstood.

Saul, the current king of Israel, had deep problems in his life which
became apparent soon after he had been appointed. He was a deeply
insecure person and, like all insecure people, tried to compensate for his
failings by such things as people-pleasing, attention-getting and so on.
One day, when returning from a battle with the Philistines in company
with David, he heard the women singing a song they had put together
in honour of the victory: 'Saul has slain his thousands, and David his
tens of thousands' (1 Sam. 18:7). Saul was deeply upset. It was not just
the numerical difference that bothered him, but the fact that David was
getting the glory: 'What more can he get but the kingdom?' (v.8).

But David was not after the kingdom. He was Saul's man, and
amongst other things his personal musician. The innocent acts of David
were so misinterpreted by Saul that thereafter David's life became
almost unbearable. If it's any comfort, being misunderstood, it seems,
has always been the standard operating procedure for those whom
God appoints to special service. You do not grow fully or completely
without being misunderstood.

**Father, I see that though misunderstanding sometimes causes me to groan, it
also causes me to grow. Help me to come through all my own misunderstandings
a better, not a bitter, person. For Your own dear name's sake. Amen.**

HANDLING MISUNDERSTANDING

FOR READING AND MEDITATION – PSALM 140:1–13

'I said to the Lord, You are my God; give ear to the voice
of my supplications, O Lord.' (v.6, Amplified)

MANY BIBLE COMMENTATORS believe that the psalm before
us today was written by David following the events we discussed
yesterday. David is now on the run and being hunted by an angry King
Saul. An explanation of this psalm brings out some principles which
ought to help us next time we are misunderstood.

The first thing to notice is that David recognised his predicament had
been caused by exaggeration. When people misunderstand you, they
exaggerate what you said or what you did and make it mean something
you did not intend. Look how exaggeration affected David's enemies:
'They devise mischiefs in their heart; continually they gather together
and stir up wars' (v.2, Amplified). Often misunderstanding starts with
a slightly wrong interpretation and then gradually builds up to the
point where a person is willing to believe out-and-out lies.

Next, David got in touch with his feelings and acknowledged his
sense of vulnerability: 'Keep me, O LORD, from the hands of the
wicked' (v.4). These are the words of a person who feels vulnerable and
exposed. Vulnerability is one of the things that reverberates inside us
whenever we are misunderstood. We are caught off our guard, we are
not prepared or ready to deal with it, we feel trapped, naked, exposed.
What do we do when this sort of thing happens? Look at the passage
again: 'I said to the Lord, You are my God' (v.6, Amplified). Notice,
he *said* this to the Lord, he did not just think it. Our dependence on
God must be verbalised if it is to be realised. Talking to Him not only
gets something out of us; it opens us up to God so that He might get
something into us.

O Father, help me see the importance of talking to You about my problems.
Show me even more clearly how verbalising my thoughts opens up my inner
being and prepares me to receive. In Jesus' name I pray. Amen.

WE ARE NOT ORPHANS

FOR READING AND MEDITATION – PROVERBS 16:1–16

'When a man's ways are pleasing to the Lord, he makes
even his enemies live at peace with him.' (v.7)

WE RETURN TODAY to the thought that we can actually grow
through misunderstanding. It hurts when it happens, but it has a
way of causing us to depend on the Lord in a way that perhaps we
have never quite done before. Once we give the situation over to God
and say: 'Lord, I have done what I know is right, but I feel defenceless
and misunderstood', then we must wait and let Him vindicate us.
His ability to vindicate, as our text for today suggests, is one of our
Creator's specialities!

Are you misunderstood in your home or your place of work?
Is someone in your school, college or university causing you hurt
through an innocent remark that you might have made? Then ask
Jesus to be your defence. Don't just think it – talk to Him about it. Ask
Him to take care of you and then you can lie down at night knowing
that although the tongue of your accuser might be busy, God is taking
care of the situation. Far too many of us forget that when we become
Christians, we enter into the family of God. We have a new Father who
delights in taking care of our needs and becoming involved in every
detail of our lives. We are not orphans, we are children of the living
God. So learn to bring all your misunderstandings to Him.

Early in my ministry I was involved in a situation where I was so
misunderstood that I thought the pain would never go away. Crushed
and bruised, all I could do was wait. The memory of the event is still
there, but the sting has gone and something very beautiful has come
out of it. I would not give a penny for the pain, but I would not take a
million pounds for what has emerged in my life because of it.

O God my Father, help me to grow gracefully, beautifully and creatively.
Let everything that happens to me be used to increase Your likeness in me.
For Jesus' sake. Amen.

'WHEN OTHER HELPERS FAIL ...'

FOR READING AND MEDITATION – JOHN 14:1–14

'Philip said, "Lord, show us the Father and
that will be enough for us."' (v.8)

PROBABLY NO ONE in history was more misunderstood than Jesus Christ. He came to earth offering love, pouring it out passionately and prodigally on all who were in need, but the more He ministered, the more He was misunderstood. The people among whom He had been brought up misunderstood Him. His own immediate family misunderstood Him. Even His disciples, who spent so much time in His presence and knew Him more closely than any others – they, too, misunderstood Him at times. Although the text before us today cannot strictly be put under the category of misunderstanding, it must have grieved Jesus greatly that, even though Philip had been with Him almost from the first day of His public ministry, he had not really understood the Master's purpose in the world or who He was. 'Show us the Father,' said Philip, 'that is all we ask; then we shall be satisfied' (v.8, Amplified).

How these words must have hurt the heart of Jesus. Philip had listened to His words, witnessed the many miracles He had performed, seen first-hand the demonstration of Deity, yet he still had not grasped the relationship of Christ to God. It's like an art student studying under the tutorship of an art master for three years, then suddenly turning to him at the end of the time and saying, 'Please show me the principles of art.' Let me make the point once again – when it comes to the issue of being misunderstood or not being understood (there is a slight difference between the two), remember that no one has touched this as deeply as Jesus. Take comfort in the thought that when other helpers fail and comforts flee – there is always Jesus.

Blessed Lord Jesus, forgive me that so often I look to You as the last resource
for comfort rather than the first. Help me to be a more dependent person –
God-dependent. In Your name I ask it. Amen.

 **LIVING TH**

ICEBREAKERS

• What emotions would a child who has lost his or her favourite comforter or blanket experience?

• Can you share any details of a personal time of loss or grief?

FOR GROUP DISCUSSION

• Review the words of Matt Redman's song 'Blessed be Your name …' and Job's response to his own loss.

• How do you deal with the emotions of loss and grief?

ʒH LOSS AND GRIEF

- Describe how we respond to God in times of grief?

- How can we relate to those experiencing loss and grief?

- Discuss the process of dealing with prolonged or excessive grief.

- How did Jesus deal with grief?

- How can we express our grief without being dragged down by our feelings into a whirlpool of despair?

PRAYER

Jesus, I remember that You are the One who wept at the grave of Your dearest friend. You not only know how I feel, but You make available to me Your unfailing strength, love and understanding to accompany me and help me in my grief. Amen.

'TRUST MY LOVE'

FOR READING AND MEDITATION – JEREMIAH 15:10–21

'Why is my pain unending and my wound grievous and incurable?' (v.18)

HAVING EXPLORED HOW Jesus experienced loss we turn now to focus on another aspect of the way in which Jesus has identified with our humanity – the aspect of suffering and pain. No one has suffered more than our Lord, and His experience in Gethsemane and on the cross are evidences of this fact.

How do we begin to deal with this difficult problem of suffering and pain? It keeps raising its head, regardless of the most erudite attempts to explain it away. Even C.S. Lewis, who offered perhaps one of the most articulate explanations of it, saw his arguments wilt as he watched the onslaught of bone cancer in his wife's body. Some time later, he wrote, 'You never know how much you really believe anything until its truth or falsehood becomes a matter of life and death to you.' I know something of what he meant, having watched my wife die in a similar way. Like Hercules battling against the Hydra, all our attempts to chop down the arguments of atheists and agnostics in relation to suffering and pain are met with writhing new examples, each one seemingly worse than the others.

Is suffering and pain, as some philosophers claim, God's big mistake? I do not believe so myself. I remember as a child having to have my tonsils removed and, when the moment came to enter the hospital, I clung to my mother, pleading with her to save me from the ordeal. The look she gave me said, 'I must not save you from it. You will understand some day. You must trust my love.' This is how God deals with us in the presence of suffering and pain. He says, 'What I permit may not make much sense to you now … but there is a purpose. Trust my love!'

O Father, in my moments of perplexity when I struggle with this issue of suffering and pain, help me realise that the One who asks for my trust is the One who gave Himself for me on Calvary. In the light of this, how can I hold back? Amen.

IF YOU WERE GOD ...

FOR READING AND MEDITATION – GENESIS 1:1–31

**'Then God said, "Let us make man in our
image, in our likeness ..."' (v.26)**

WE CONTINUE THINKING through the issue of suffering and pain. Omnipotence, of course, could have easily avoided the problem but only at the price of making us marionettes. Can anyone who is not utterly engulfed in sorrow regret that God did not take that path; that His love would not compromise with sin; that nothing would thwart Him in His purpose of giving us freedom of will? But, by giving us free will, God had to take the risk that we would misuse and misapply our freedom.

One writer uses this analogy to describe the situation: God made wood, which is a useful product as the branches of a tree bear fruit, support leaves that provide us with shade and shelter birds and other forms of wildlife. Even taken from the tree, wood is useful. Men use it to build homes and many other useful things. Wood, however, is hard and therefore potentially dangerous. You can put a piece of wood in a man's hand and he can either use it to make something useful or break open the skull of another man. Of course, God could reach down each time a man hit another with a heavy piece of wood and turn the wood into a sponge so that the wood would bounce off lightly – but that is not what freedom is all about.

Months after C.S. Lewis's wife had died, a friend said to him while out walking, 'If you were God, would you make a man like a machine or with the freedom to choose?' He paused for a while and his sharp mind saw right through to the core of the issue. If he were a machine, he would not feel the intense pain he was going through at the time, but then he realised he would not feel joy either. His reply was short but filled with deep understanding: 'I would do as God did.'

O Father, if I were a machine I would not be able to fellowship with You. To commune with You is worth far more than any pain or suffering I may have to go through. I would have it no other way – even though 'seven deaths lay between'. Amen.

'PAIN – GOD'S MEGAPHONE'

FOR READING AND MEDITATION – REVELATION 21:1–8

'[God] will wipe every tear from their eyes.
There will be no more ... pain ...' (v.4)

IN THE DAYS prior to my conversion, one of the things that used to impress me about Christianity was its willingness to meet the issue of sin and suffering head on. Other religions set out to deny that pain exists or encouraged their adherents to deal with it stoically. Many dodged the issue of pain – Christianity looked it squarely in the face. C.S. Lewis described suffering and pain as 'God's megaphone'. It is an appropriate phrase because it shouts to us that something is wrong.

It was this aspect of Christianity that made G.K. Chesterton say, 'The modern philosopher told me I was in the right place but I still felt depressed, even in acquiescence. Then I heard that I was in the wrong place and my soul sang for joy.' What did he mean? The optimists of his day told him that this world was the best of all possible worlds and he should make the best of it. Christianity came along and told him that this is a stained, marred planet.

This perspective then led him to say, 'It entirely reversed the reason for optimism. And the instant the reversal was made, it felt like the abrupt ease when a bone is put back in the socket. I had often called myself an optimist to avoid the too evident blasphemy of pessimism. But the optimism of the age was false and disheartening because it tried to prove we have to fit into the world.' Suffering and pain, God's megaphone, can either drive us from Him or draw us to Him. It can make us angry with God for allowing such conditions in His universe, or make us appreciative of God for building a new environment in which sin and sorrow will have no place.

Gracious Father, I see I do not have to fit into this world, for You are preparing for me a new world where everything fits. Because of this I am a true optimist – one who sees things from Your point of view. Thank You, Father. Amen.

GOD HAS SUFFERED TOO!

FOR READING AND MEDITATION – HEBREWS 12:1–13

'Consider him who endured … so that you will
not grow weary and lose heart.' (v.3)

IT SEEMS ALMOST fatuous to ask the question: did Christ experience suffering and pain? In keeping with our theme, we must ask it nevertheless. Linger with me today at the foot of Calvary. One writer says of it, 'The scene, with its sharp spikes and bleeding death, has been told so often that we, who shrink from a news story on the death of baby seals, flinch not at all at its retelling.' How sad.

The physical and mental sufferings of Christ began in Gethsemane when His sweat was as great drops of blood. One doctor says, 'Though rare, this is the phenomenon of hematidrosis where, under great emotional stress, tiny capillaries in the sweat glands break, mixing blood with sweat. This process alone could have produced marked weakness and shock.' After the arrest in the middle of the night, Jesus was brought before Caiaphas the high priest, at which point a soldier struck Him across the face. The palace guards then blindfolded Him and mockingly taunted Him to identify them as they each passed by and struck Him in the face.

In the early morning, battered, bruised, dehydrated and exhausted from a sleepless night, Jesus is taken across Jerusalem to the Praetorium, where He is stripped naked and scourged. Then a heavy beam is tied to His shoulders and for a while He is forced to carry His cross until relieved of the ordeal by Simon of Cyrene. At Golgotha, He is skewered to that cross by iron nails and strung up like a dog to die. If you still struggle over the mystery as to why God allowed pain and suffering into His world, then I point you to an even greater mystery – God has suffered too!

O Father, the mystery of Your own suffering may not satisfy my reason as to why You allowed pain and suffering in Your world – but it satisfies my heart. Help me to trust You even when I cannot trace You. In Jesus' name. Amen.

'GOD CAME INCREDIBLY CLOSE'

FOR READING AND MEDITATION – LUKE 23:33–49

**'And when they had come to the place called Calvary,
there they crucified him …' (v.33, NKJV)**

THOSE WHO MAY have wondered what is meant by the phrase, 'God's wounds answer to our wounds', might find the story of what happened to Joni Eareckson Tada helpful and enlightening. One day, during the summer of 1967, Joni dived off a raft in Chesapeake Bay near Baltimore and struck her head on a rock, breaking her neck. She was instantly paralysed and, were it not for the quick thinking of a friend, might have drowned there and then. Joni was rushed to hospital and several weeks later learnt that her condition would be permanent.

Joni's spirits fell to great depths, and turning to her friend Jackie, she said, 'Help me die. Bring me some pills or a razor blade, even. I can't live inside a grotesque body like this.' Of course, Jackie couldn't bring herself to do what Joni asked, which served only to increase Joni's sense of helplessness. Some time after this, one night, while Cindy, her new-found friend, sat reading with her, Cindy blurted out, 'Joni, Jesus knows how you feel – you aren't the only one – why, He was paralysed too.' Joni asked, 'What do you mean?' 'It's true,' said Cindy. 'Remember, He was nailed on a cross. His back was raw from beatings and He must have yearned for a way to move, to change positions or redistribute His weight. But He couldn't. He was paralysed by the nails.'

The thought went deep into Joni's spirit. It had never occurred to her before that God had felt the exact piercing sensations that racked her body. 'At that moment,' said Joni, 'God came incredibly close.' This is always the effect upon those who realise that the God they serve knows exactly how they feel. May He come close, incredibly close, to you today.

Father, I am convinced of one thing, no matter how many mysteries I face in this world – You are worthy of my trust. Knowing You is worth all enduring. Thank You, my Father. Amen.

Jesus

THE RES

ICEBREAKERS

• Ask people to draw around their hand onto a sheet of paper. Mix up the papers and ask the group to guess whose hand is shown on each paper.

• What has most impacted you from our previous studies?

FOR GROUP DISCUSSION

• Discuss the implications of passages such as Matthew 9:36, 14:14, 15:32 and Mark 1:41 which record that Jesus was moved with compassion.

CTION HOPE

- Why did Jesus present Himself to common people rather than to kings and rulers? (See Luke 19:10.)

- What do the hands of Jesus reveal?

- Contrast the views of the first author (the Holocaust survivor Elie Wiesel) with those of Corrie ten Boom.

- What does the resurrection mean for us?

- Contrast the message of Christianity with that of 'religion'.

- How have these studies influenced or changed your view of Jesus and suffering?

PRAYER

Thank You, Father, that You do not leave us floundering in pain. Although You may not take the pain away, You are with us in our grief, Lord Jesus. You offer the example of how to meet suffering and give us strength and hope to face whatever comes our way. Amen.

HOW TO AVOID INFECTION

FOR READING AND MEDITATION – EPHESIANS 4:17–32

'... forgiving each other, just as in Christ God forgave you.' (v.32)

WE HAVE BEEN saying that out of the many things that endear Christ to His Church, one of the chief must be that He has worn our flesh, measured its frailty, and experienced exactly how we feel. Our Lord is a wounded healer; His ability to heal our wounds flows from the fact that He has known our wounds. Jesus has taken the entire range of our emotions with Him into the Godhead so that now our Creator feels as we feel. What a mystery!

It is important now to note the way Jesus responded to the wounds He received compared to the way, generally speaking, we respond to our wounds. When we are wounded, our natural response is either to nurse our hurt in an attitude of self-pity, or flare up in unrighteous anger. Comb the record of Jesus' days on this earth and you will not find one ounce of self-pity. When the daughters of Jerusalem wept over Him on His way to the cross, He said, 'Do not weep for me; weep for yourselves and for your children' (Luke 23:28); no self-pity.

Neither did He harbour unforgiveness. When men laid His weary body upon a cross and transfixed Him to the wood, the cry that rose from His heart was not for justice, but forgiveness: 'Father, forgive them, for they do not know what they are doing' (Luke 23:34). That was the most sublime prayer that was ever prayed, for it embodied the most sublime spirit ever shown. The cross shows us how Jesus dealt with hate. He held it to Him and quelled it in His mighty heart of love. The boomerang lost its power because the venom which flew towards Him at the crucifixion did not fly back again in revenge. He freely forgave those who hurt Him – so must we.

Blessed Lord Jesus, help me to avail myself of Your grace and power so that I, too, might be free from corroding hate and cancerous resentments. Save me, not from hurt but from infected hurts. In Your dear name I pray. Amen.

'GO HOME AND SUFFER'

FOR READING AND MEDITATION – 2 CORINTHIANS 1:1–11

'... when others are troubled ... we can pass on to them this
same help and comfort God has given us.' (v.4, TLB)

NOT ONLY IS Jesus a wounded healer, but we are called to be wounded healers also. Just as Jesus' wounds give Him a special empathy for us in our struggles and sorrows, so our own wounds can be used to soothe and strengthen those who hurt. For example, it is well known in the field of counselling that often the best helpers are those who have suffered deep hurt themselves and have found a way through it.

Some time ago, I saw a video tape of Rollo May, a well-known counsellor in the United States, and I remember being deeply impressed with a statement he made which I cannot quote verbatim but which went something like this: 'Whenever I interview anyone who wants to join my team as a counsellor, the first thing I have to know is how much they have suffered. If they cannot convince me that they have experienced some suffering, then I tell them I have no use for them at the moment and to come back when they have really suffered.'

Strong words – but understandable. Very often, the more we have suffered, the more our sufferings can speak to others. And remember, you don't have to be a trained counsellor to help others. Every Christian has something he or she can offer to a brother or sister who is hurting if, as our text for today points out, we let God comfort us and then pass on the same comfort to others. Shakespeare put it well when he said, 'He jests at scars who never felt a wound.' Believe me, there is no more powerful ministry than to come alongside someone who is suffering and share with them the fact that you have felt that self-same hurt too. Your weakness, under God, becomes someone else's strength.

Father, I am beginning to understand that no hurt is wasted. When I hurt, I can know Your comfort, and that comfort I can pass on to others, as one who truly empathises. Help me to be a wounded healer like Your Son. Amen.

SUFFERING VERSUS MIRACLES

FOR READING AND MEDITATION – JOHN 5:16–30

'... the Son can do nothing by himself; he can only
do what he sees his Father doing ...' (v.19)

WE HAVE BEEN emphasising that we are to welcome suffering and see it as an opportunity to take the sympathy and empathy we receive from Jesus and pass it on to others. But now, the question may be raised in some people's minds: where is the place for miracles in all this? Is life all suffering? Doesn't God promise to deliver us from some things and work supernaturally on our behalf?

Of course He does. There are many situations where faith in God brings great deliverance, so don't hear me discounting the place of prayer and miracles in Christian life. After all, God is a big God and delights in answering prayer. That said, however, it is clear that even in the most charismatic of churches, where miracles and supernatural happenings abound, there is still a good deal of suffering. People get hurt, things go wrong, and troubles come, as Shakespeare said, 'not single spies but in battalions'.

What do we do when, despite the most positive and energetic intercession, we continue to experience hurt and anguish and sorrow? We turn to God and draw from our great 'El Shaddai' (literally 'The Breasted One') strength and encouragement. If you do not get these two things in perspective – miracles and suffering – you will finish up greatly confused. God does work miracles in answer to prayer, but at times He chooses to let us pass through something so that He can use it in our lives to deepen our understanding and enrich our ministry to others. As Alan Paton puts it in his book *Cry, the Beloved Country*, 'Christ suffered, not just to save us from suffering, but to teach us how to use it'.

Loving and gracious heavenly Father, help me to have a clear perspective on this issue of suffering versus miracles. Help me to know when You want to keep me from something and when You want to keep me in something. In Christ's name. Amen.

TURNING PAINS INTO PEARLS

FOR READING AND MEDITATION – REVELATION 21:9–27

'... each gate made of a single pearl.' (v. 21)

IT IS QUITE clear from what we have been seeing over the past few days that Christians are to follow in the steps of Jesus and turn their sufferings to good account. The way in which this is to be done is beautifully illustrated by the experience of the oyster, into whose shell there comes one day a grain of sand. This tiny piece of quartz lies there imposing pain and stress – so what shall the oyster do?

There are several courses open. The oyster could, as so many men and women have done in times of adversity, openly rebel against God. The oyster, metaphorically speaking, could shake a fist in God's face and say, 'Why should this happen to me?' Or it could say, 'It can't be true; this is not happening to me. I must not permit myself to believe it.' It could say also, 'There is no such thing as pain. It is an error of the mind. I must think positive thoughts.' But the oyster does none of these things.

What, then, does it do? Slowly and patiently, and with infinite care, the oyster builds upon the grain of sand layer upon layer of a white milky substance that covers every sharp corner and coats every cutting edge. And gradually ... slowly ... by and by, a pearl is made. The oyster has learned – by the will of God – to turn grains of sand into pearls. And that is the lesson we must learn along this pilgrim way. Surely it is something more than a simile when the Bible says that the entrance into the New Jerusalem is through a gate made of pearl. It is pointing out that the way into the city of God is through a wound that has been healed. Let God help you turn your pains into pearls, so that others can walk through them into joy and encouragement.

O Father, help me to turn every wound in my life into a 'pearly gate' – something through which others can pass to find faith, hope and love. In Christ's peerless and precious name I ask it. Amen.

HE'S BEEN THERE!

FOR READING AND MEDITATION – HEBREWS 12:1–11

'Let us fix our eyes on Jesus ... who for the joy set
before him endured the cross ...' (v.2)

IN THE BOOK *Migrants, Sharecroppers and Mountaineers*, Robert Coles tells the story of a migrant worker whose daughter was seriously ill, and one morning in church he strode up to the minister, lifted up his daughter and shouted, 'My daughter is sick and we have no money to help her. How can you talk about a God who loves when He takes good care of some and not of people like us?'

That migrant worker summed up the dilemma about suffering about as well as it can be expressed. Why does God allow a world of sick children, of poverty and of little hope? I don't have a clear answer for this problem and nor, I suspect, do you. But I know one thing – the God who made the world has been here and seen for Himself what it is like to suffer. He took on the same flesh that you have. His nerve fibres were not bionic – they screamed with pain when misused. There is nothing known to us which He has not felt. And that one fact makes all the difference:

When we come to the place of full retreat
And our heart cries out for God
The only person whose heart ours can meet
Is the one who has likewise trod
Others may offer a word of cheer
To lift us from despair
But above the rest, the one we hear,
Is the whisper, 'I've been there.'

Take heart. No matter what your struggles, your Lord has been there!

O Jesus, Master of the inward wound, teach us the same mastery. Help me to go on when wounded by life, knowing that Your wounds are answering my wounds. And may my wounds answer someone else's wounds. For Your own dear name's sake. Amen.

* C.R. Solomon, *Handbook to Happiness* (Wheaton, Il.: Tyndale House Publishers, 1976). Used by permission of C.R. Solomon.

Discover the basic laws that govern your spiritual life

Explore seven key spiritual principles to be followed for a successful and effective Christian life.

Through these eight deeply challenging, 20-minute sessions* you will gain:

- Kingdom priorities
- A more positive outlook
- Greater perseverance

and much more of God's presence and power in your life.

Presented by CWR's Mick Brooks in various locations including a maze, a police cell and a glider!

Ideal for individual or small-group study.

This DVD is based on the bestselling book by Selwyn Hughes, *7 Laws of Spiritual Success* and includes questions for group discussion on screen for each session.

Available online at www.cwr.org.uk/store or by calling 01252 784700.
Also available in many Christian bookshops.

*Approximate time.

7 Laws for Life DVD
Presented by Mick Brooks | Content by Selwyn Hughes
Format: DVD PAL
EAN: 5027957001114